CRAP MY STUDENTS MAKE

And Other Teacher Misery

Пн Вт Ср Чт Пт Сб Вс

FOR M,

Always for you

And for the teachers who
last more than five years,
You're fucking saints.

And for the teachers who
last more than twenty
years,
You're fucking maniacs.

INTRODUCTION

If you don't learn to laugh you'll be crying a lot of the time. That's the best advice I can give to anyone in the teaching profession. (It's pretty good advice for parents as well.) There is so much absurdity that goes on in school each and every day, and a lot of it is downright hilarious, if you choose to see it that way.

Grading papers is horrible. It is painfully boring. Every time I give an assignment I have 150+ to read. That means that a large portion of my life is spent reading literary analyses written by unwilling teenagers. I live for the responses that are so outrageous, ridiculous, inappropriate or just plain stupid that I laugh til I cry. I have such gratitude for the students who are bold enough to just go for it! The ones who say to themselves, "I have no idea what I'm doing so I'm just gonna say fuck it and have some fun." Some of the most successful people in history have lived by this philosophy. I respect it. It's how Teacher Misery was born.

When a kid writes "I don't know I don't really care" as his entire final exam essay, you have to step back and respect his boldness and raw honesty. Kids are trained to bullshit their

...ay through school and this kid isn't willing to play the game. He'll end up the CEO of his own successful company or getting fired from Subway for spitting in the mayo. It really could go either way.

Teenagers are angry, impulsive, irrational and impossible but they also channel that craziness in some really interesting ways. It's fascinating to watch.

Teenagers write funny shit on purpose, to amuse themselves or to get some much needed attention (except for the ones who genuinely don't know that douchebag is an inappropriate word for a formal essay. Bless their hearts.) But younger kids make mistakes and create things that are so raw, honest and genuine that you have to cherish it. Ask any teacher and they will tell you that they save the funny stuff forever. The thank you cards are nice, but the drawing of the teacher complete with titties and pubes? That goes into the SAVE FOREVER file.

The best part of my job, and one of the only reasons I do it, is how funny it is. It makes my whole life better. I have the best stories at dinner parties and I'm ready to start my standup career at any time. The absurdity of my job has become a part of who I am. And I really like that.

NOTE
everything in
this book is
100%
authentic.

Work Cited
"extremely creditable resources"

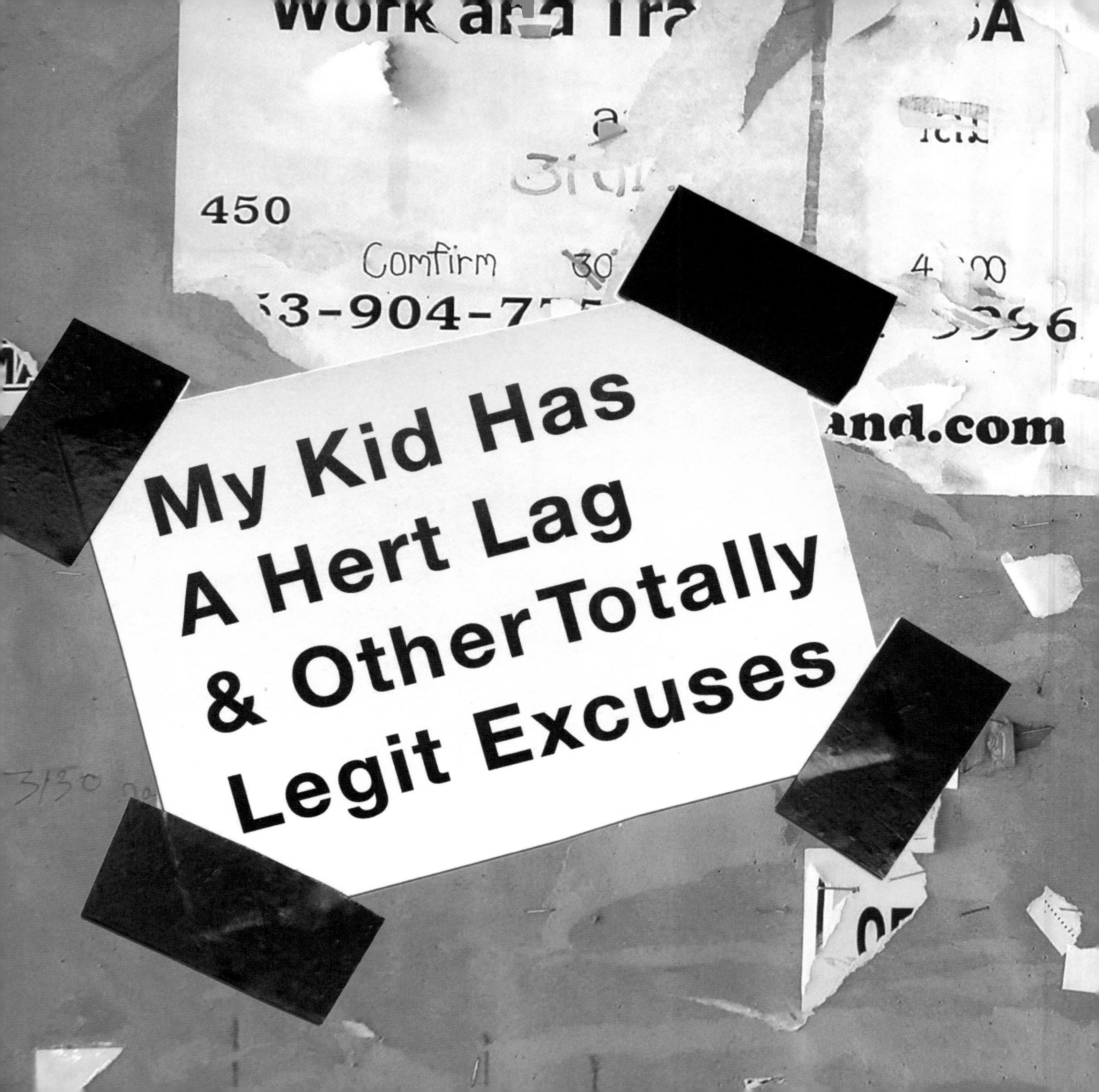
My Kid Has
A Hert Lag
& Other Totally
Legit Excuses

the school compny is taking
a brake so the kids will get one
more week of school off and we
will need your child to sign
their name here ↓
cara G.
_____

1. Ben's pet dog, ~~~~
~~~~ the wet grass and Ben
~~~~ grass with him. Ben fell
~~~~ chin on a big clump of
~~~~ blunt cut on his lip. Still,
~~~~ m with Tom. At last they

Read to an
adult 2 times.

dad
Adult Signature

Hope her
lag feels
better
soon!

Mikaila can not
do P. E. because
she has a hert lag

Today I went to red becc~~

I chose to use my hands and/or feet to hurt others.

I chose not to stay in my seat.

I chose not to follow directions the first time.

I chose not to raise my hand to speak (interrupting).

I chose to be disrespectful to my teacher, classmate(s), or another adult

I chose to act silly and play at an inappropriate time.

I chose to waste time and not finish my work.

I chose to not pay attention and distract others while my teacher was teachi~~

I chose to misbehave at lunch.

I chose to misbehave at gym, music or art.

I chose to misbehave at recess.

sary she did that she w~~
~~~ not do it agan are ~~~
~~~ talk to your student about the highlighted area~~
~~~ciate your support.
sins dad

Parent Signature

FROM
THE OFFICE
OF THE
SUPERINTENDENT
...OBVIOUSLY.

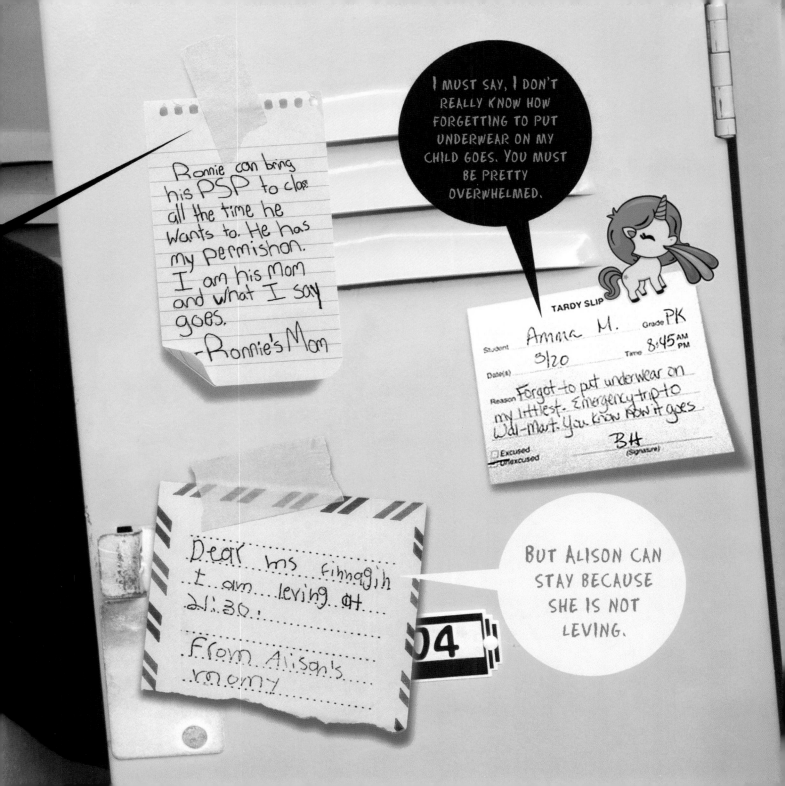

Dear Mrs Miller
Ray is so sick he cannot go to school.
Rays Mom
No homework plese
DEAR RAYS MOM, I WON'T SEND ANY HOMEWORK IF YOU STOP SENDING SHITTY NOTES PLESE.
This student has 88hd so he can use a fidget spinner Mrs Dickingson
Doctor + Caleb
DEAR DOCTOR + CALEB, I WOULD LIKE TO HELP CALEB LEARN TO MANAGE HIS 88HD BY BURNING HIS FIDGET SPINNER INTO A MOUND OF USELESS MUCK.

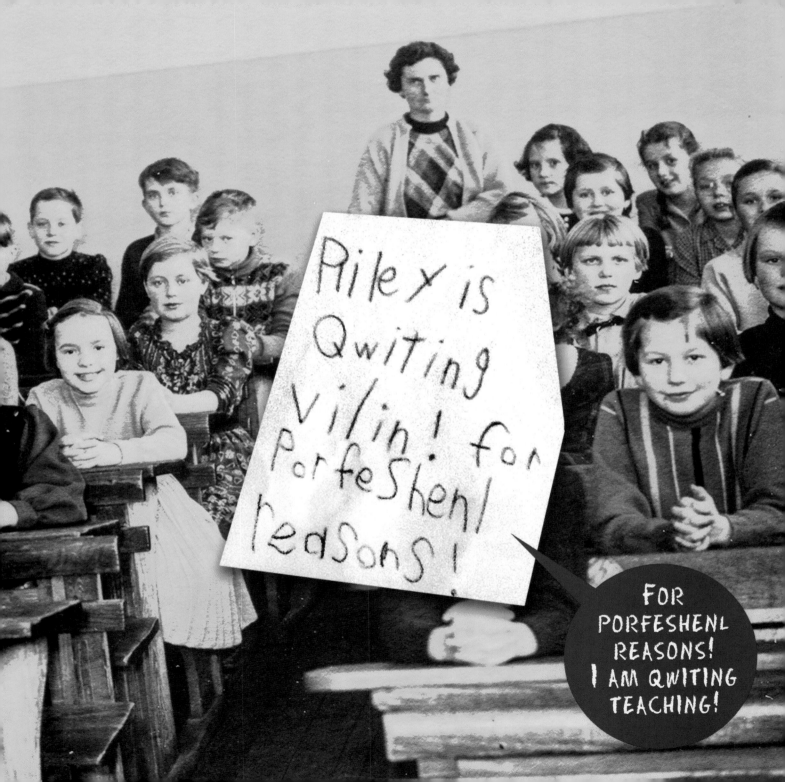

WINTER JUST GOT
A WHOLE LOT
SEXIER!

"WHISTLE"

"scissors"

"CAR"

"MICROPHONE"

"DINOSAUR"

"NOSE"

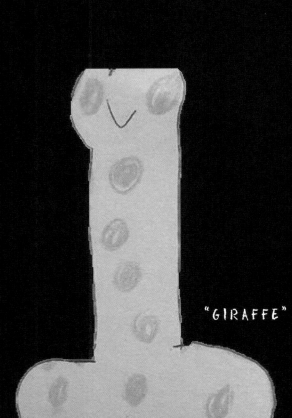

"GIRAFFE"

"SHADOW"

"LIGHTHOUSE

"COKE CAN"

"HAT"

?

"POLAR BEAR"

"CAT"

"LEG/FOOT"

"VOLCANO"

"DON'T STOP BELIEVING,
UNLESS YOUR DREAM IS STUPID."
-KID PRESIDENT

When I grow up I want to be a scientist. because I like to discover new things. and its fun to do. I can be one of the first people to be a girl scientist. or I might work at Pazsa hut because my brother use tio work there and he got free Pazsa to take home. and that is what I want to be when I grow up.

3. My favorite thing to do in my free time is _lay down_

4. My favorite TV show is _I dk_.

5. When I grow up, I want to be a _A hustler_.

6. If I had a million dollars, I would _spend it_.

"Do not follow
where the path
may lead.
Go instead
where there is
no path and
leave a trail."
—RALPH WALDO
EMERSON

When I Grow Up
I'd like to be...

Toby - a veterinarian so I can help pets get better
Sophia - a baseball player because baseball is fun.
Albert - a person who stays home and does nothing.

My one wish is...
for it to rain
tacos

one question for my teacher:
who
s

"Start where you are. Use what you have. Do what you can."
—ARTHUR ASHE

I have [2] siblings.
I have [0] pets.
I want to be a
couch potato
when I grow up.

My goals for this year...
not to have goal

what do you want to be when you grow up?

I want to be a wolf.

At the end of the rainbow there is a Toko Bell.

"Never limit yourself because of others' limited imagination; never limit others because of your own limited imagination."
—MAE JEMISON

"Hold fast to dreams for if dreams die, life is a broken-winged bird that cannot fly."
—LANGSTON HUGHES

I am interested in these career fields:
1. Nursing
2. Teaching
3. Stripping
4.

I'll be famous one day but for now I'm stuck in 2nd grade with a bunch of morons

"The future belongs to those who believe in the beauty of their dreams."
—ELEANOR ROOSEVELT

When I grow up I
want to be a JCPENNY
Store.

"Always remember, you have within you the strength, the patience, and the passion to reach for the stars to change the world."
—HARRIET TUBMAN

I want to be a persun who cleans tables

I will one day be a potatoe

"Believe in your greatness. Because what you believe is what you become."
—UDAI YADLA

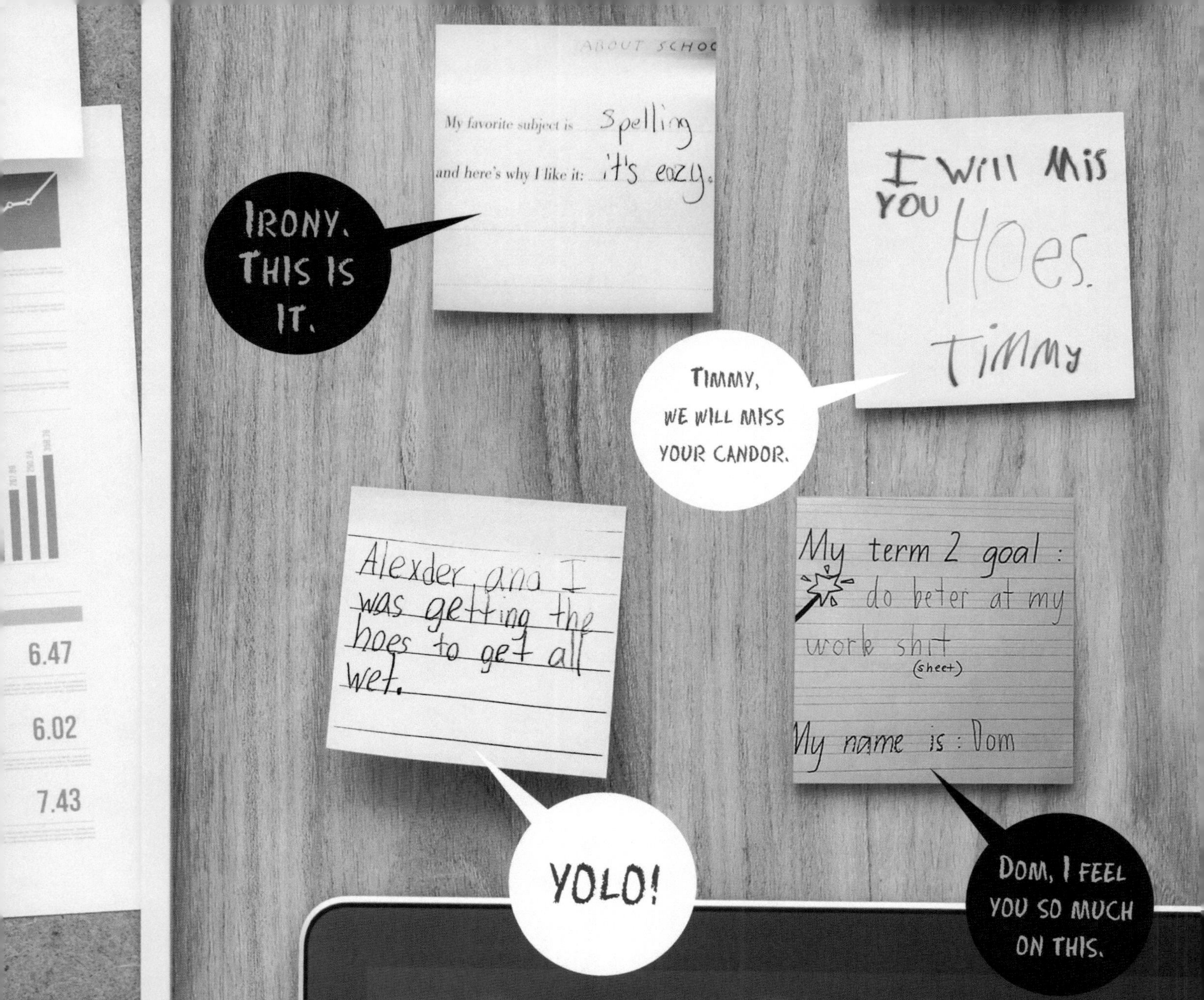

"I Cum in Pies" & other Misspellings

1. My dick is made of hard wood!

2. My dick is very big.

3. My mother says only my freinds can sit on my dick?

Michael,
Great sentences!.
The word is deck

10. Name a sound that is **pleasant** sounding to you. Explain why you find it pleasant.

a relaxing song. that make yo
come.

Please God, tell me this kid meant to write "CALM."

That is definitely the most interesting superpower I have ever heard of!

9-25

I think ironman is the best superhero because he can shit lazers.

h state is the birthplace of the most Presidents? _____ Vagina

many Presidents were born in Texas (TX)? _____ 2

Presidents were born in which state? _____ Ohio

This Vagina place sounds pretty amazing.

5. concert
6. Massassetts
7. Maryland
8. south vagina
9. Vermonk
10. conetu
11. New York
12. North vagina
13. Rhode Island

Tomorrow I am not going to be here because I am going to be in Vagina

The ABCs of Me
Natalie

A - APPETITE: PIZZA
B - BEST CHILDHOOD MEMORY: FLORIDA
C - CHARITY: I GAVE FOOD TO THE POOR
D - DREAM: TO HAVE NO UNIFORM
E - ESSENTIAL START TO YOUR DAY: TO HAVE BREAKFAS
F - FEAR: SPIDERS
G - GREAT PLACE TO VISIT: VAGINA
H - HAIR: BLOND
I - INTERESTING JOB: SCIENTIST J - JUICE: APPLE JUIC
K - KINDNESS: HELPFUL
L - LAUGHTER: FUNNY WORDS
M - MEAL: DINNER
N - NUT: PUSTASHEO
O - OLIVES: I LIKE OLIVES
P - PET PEEVE: BROTHER
Q - QUOTE: HAPPY
R - REGION: PARK

Name: VIVIAN

test

At first I was shocked, but now I'm just confused.

I like my new
tits.
my tits are cats

I repeat, what you do in your personal time is none of my business.

I like to play
with my pube

I whacketitoff.

I'll be sure to avoid the pies, thanks.

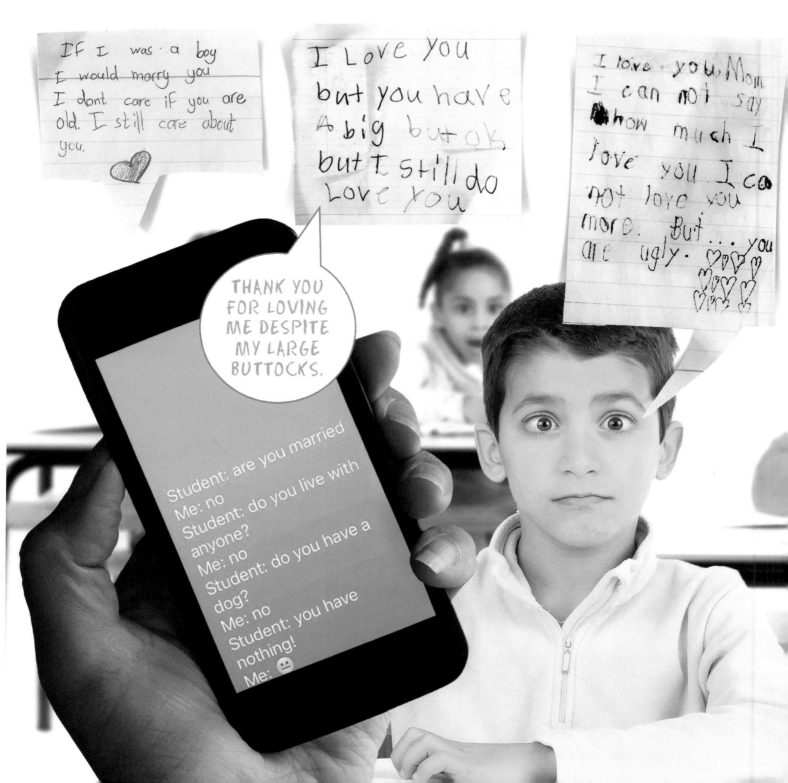

Dear Mrs Twit,
I think you should get plastic surgery so it would fix your nose. I think you need to go to the dentist becaurse it would fix your crooked teeth. Also have good thoughts, so your face will look good.
From: Dan
DEAR DAN, PERHAPS I SHOULD JUST CRAWL INTO A HOLE AND STAY THERE FOREVER SO NO ONE WILL HAVE TO LOOK AT ME?
Kids don't care if you are ugly or old. They will love you in spite of this.
Me on the First Day of School

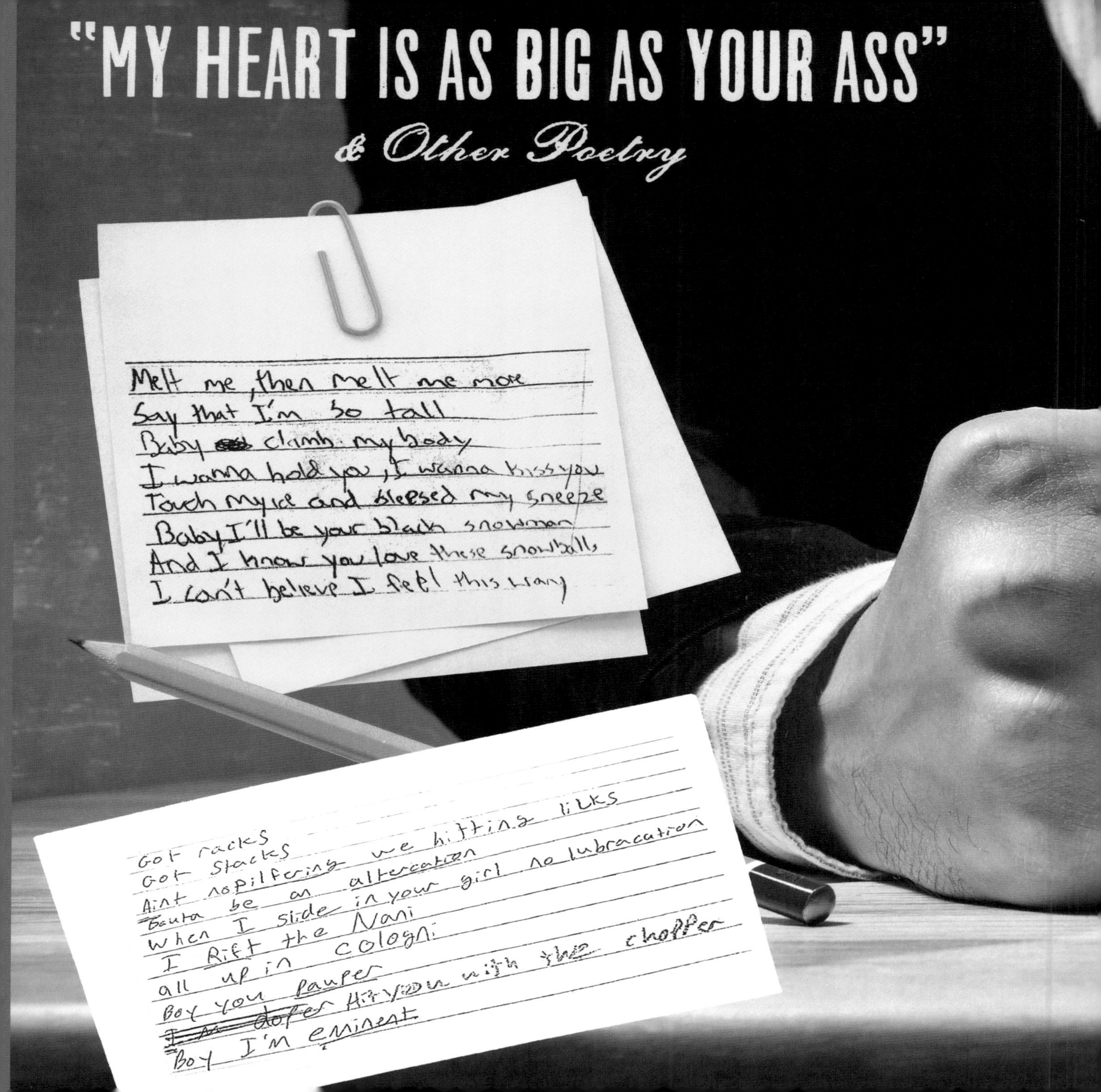
"MY HEART IS AS BIG AS YOUR ASS"
& Other Poetry
Melt me, then melt me more
Say that I'm so tall
Baby climb my body
I wanna hold you, I wanna kiss you
Touch my ice and blessed my sneeze
Baby I'll be your black snowman
And I know you love these snowballs
I can't believe I feel this way
Got racks
Got stacks
Aint no pilfering we hitting licks
Bouta be an altercation
When I slide in your girl no lubracation
I Rift the Nani
all up in cologni
Boy you pauper
I'm doper Hit you with the chopper
Boy I'm eminent

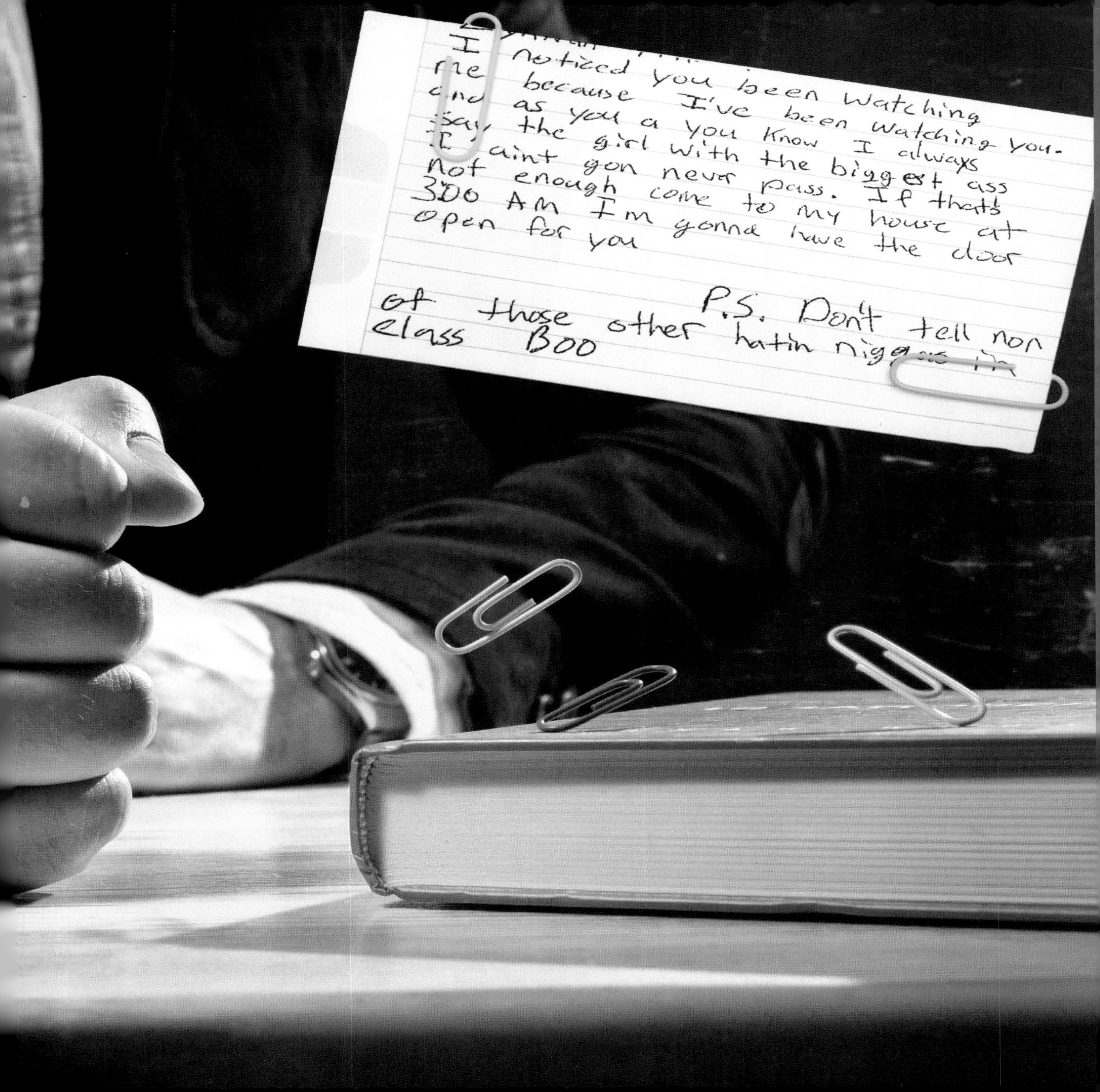
I noticed you been watching
me because I've been watching you.
and as you a you know I always
say the girl with the biggest ass
I aint gon never pass. If that's
not enough come to my house at
300 AM I'm gonna have the door
open for you
P.S. Don't tell non
of those other hatin niggas in
class Boo

"HAIKU -4-U

"Love tap" my ass,
You kicked my (beautiful head)
I don't call that love

HAIKU-BACK-2-U ★
Love is very tough.
I cannot help my spasms
I have condition.♥

Are you
a fart cuz
you just blew
me away

Dear mom
roses are red
violets are bluc
can you get me
a xbox. one
or I will stink
up your room.
P.S: X does not
mart the spot.

You make me feel so safe, Jessica.
So warm. I want to crawl up inside
you. Like Luke Skywalker crawled
up inside his tauntaun to protect
himself from the sub-zero
temperatures of Hoth, where the
Rebel Alliance was hiding from
the Galactic Empire.

Jaime, i've been thinking about you for so
long, i wish you could be mine, will you be my valentine?
your sweet like sugar, and hot like tea baby, your thighs
are like an elephant, big, juicy, giving me more cusion
for the pushing, I love you with all my heart, and my
heart is big, like your ass

Your secret admirer

Condoms, dildo's, handcuffs, and lube,
please grant me the touch of your pube,
prehistoric, middle ages, renaissance,
ITALY, Germany, or France,
I'm only for YOU!

Ratchet ass girl you dont need
love and affection, 12 baby daddies
you need some damn protection
eww girl you stank
P.S. I Love You

"Sorry I Pooped on the Playground"

& OTHER HEARTFELT LETTERS

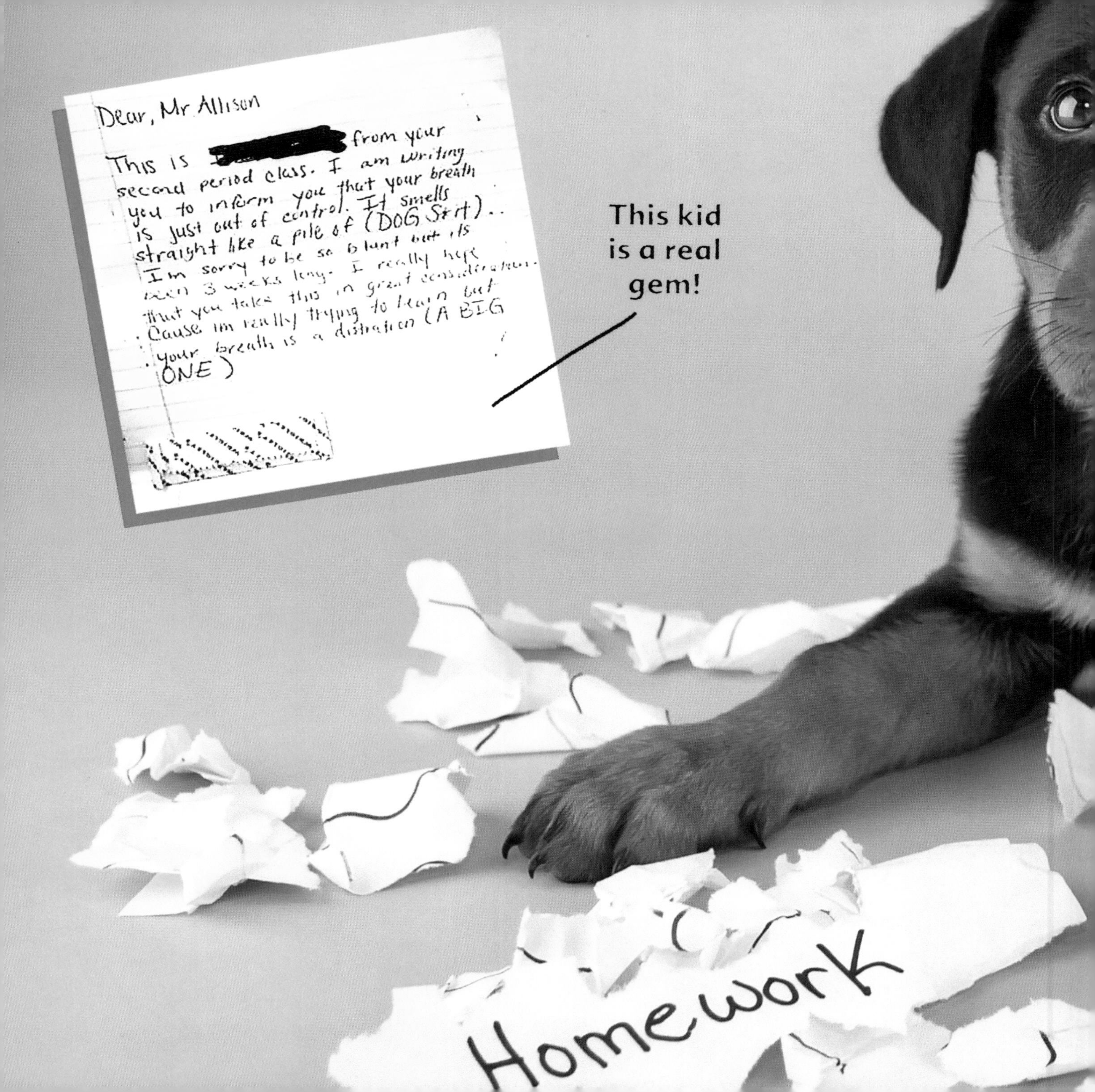

Mrs. Baum,
I am sorry I wiped my Boogers on my homework. May I have an new homework please
I'll just give you the credit. Please go away.
Thank you for being the best teacher ever! I think you are the best teacher ever because all my other teachers tell my mom and dad that I need drugs, and you did not. You allso teach very well.
Happy to be of service.
Thanks for Being such a great teacher and teaching us stuff that I forgot already, from Ben
Well Ben, remembering things was sort of what I was going for but thanks!
You're a good student but not my most favorite.
Your a good teacher but not my most favoarite

I am sorry Ben I didnt mean to hurt you. I feel like crap. I love you and I was trying to hit chris. I hate Chris. I hate my choice I made. I rally hope you except my apologee. when I throo the Sizzors I was aiming for chris I hope you start to feel better soon

Sorry! I was trying to maim Chris!

Your Zoo is a jaiL. The cages are to small Tigger Was crYing.

I hate the visit.

Tell me how you really feel.

Ben ⌉ Love
Chris ⌉ hate

I'm sorry for pooping in the playground

It's cool.
I have two dogs.
I'm used to it.

Ms ▮▮▮▮
You are so pretty. You are so so beautiful. You are so so so sexc. I love your boobs and but

At first I was like 😊 *but then I was like* 😟

Dear Mr.

You were the best teacher a student could ever have! I love my class too! I am sad that I'm going to second grade. If I had a choise between you getting killed and my favroite tree geting choped down, I will choose my favroite tree getting choped down.

That is truly touching and a bit horrifying.

PORTRAITS OF THE TEACHER

"BIRTHDAY GIFT CAUSES BLADDER MALFUNTION" 2013 MARKER ON CONSTRUCTION PAPER

"LEAVE NOTHING TO THE IMAGINATION" 2014 CRAYON ON WORKSHEET

My First Da...

"ALL THE IMPORTANT PARTS"
2016
CRAYON AND PENCIL ON CONSTRUCTION PAPER

"TEACHER AS MEAN, RAVENOUS PIRATE"
2015
MARKER AND PENCIL ON PAPER

you is mean

"MY TEACHER AS BASIC SHAPES"
2014
CRAYON ON PAPER

My Teacher

MS. Wallace

"LOW HANGING RACK OR SUPER HIGH ASS?"
2017
PENCIL ON PHOTOCOPIED PAPER

"MY TEACHER AS TRI-BOOB WITH A CRAZY EYE"
2016
MARKER ON PAPER

"IT'S A MINIONS SHIRT I SWEAR!"
2014
CONSTRUCTION PAPER AND YARN

"HOW TO TWERK"

& OTHER SCHOLARLY ESSAYS

After reading the first paragraph of whatever the fuck this essay is titled, my initial response would be that you are either a bit unstable or you are trying to fail my class on purpose.

    After reading the 1st chapter of whatever the fuck this book it's titled, my initial response would be that I retained almost no information due to the fact that I have spent almost three nights now working on your godforsaken first project. Now initially I was going to fall asleep at around 2:13 but then a little light bulb went off. I hadn't done the reading. After drawing line and lines and lines and lines for what seemed like an eternity I still had to sit down and try to soak up as much information as I could before I passed out. As I started reading and realized that lines were

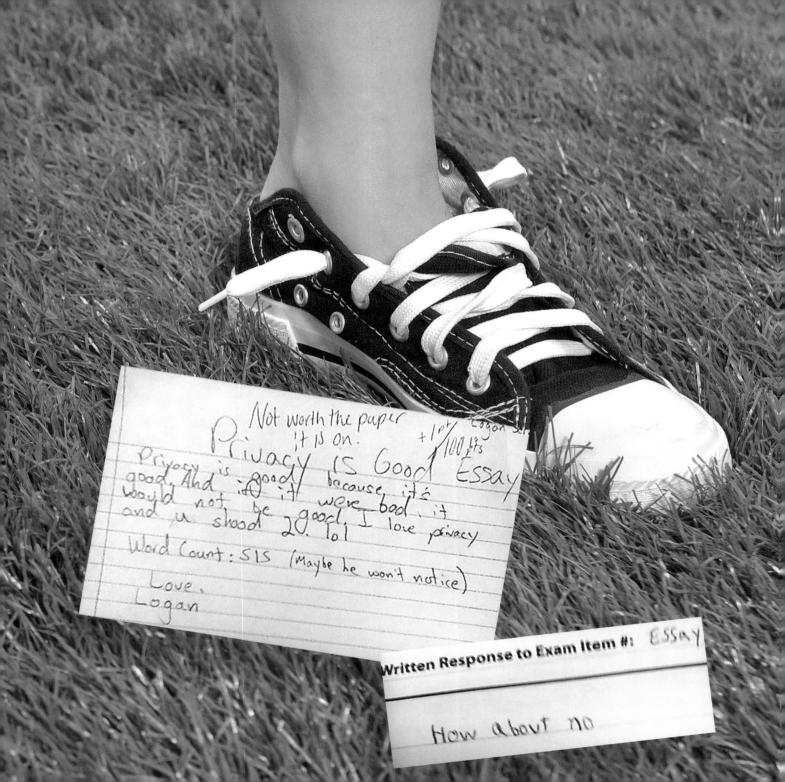

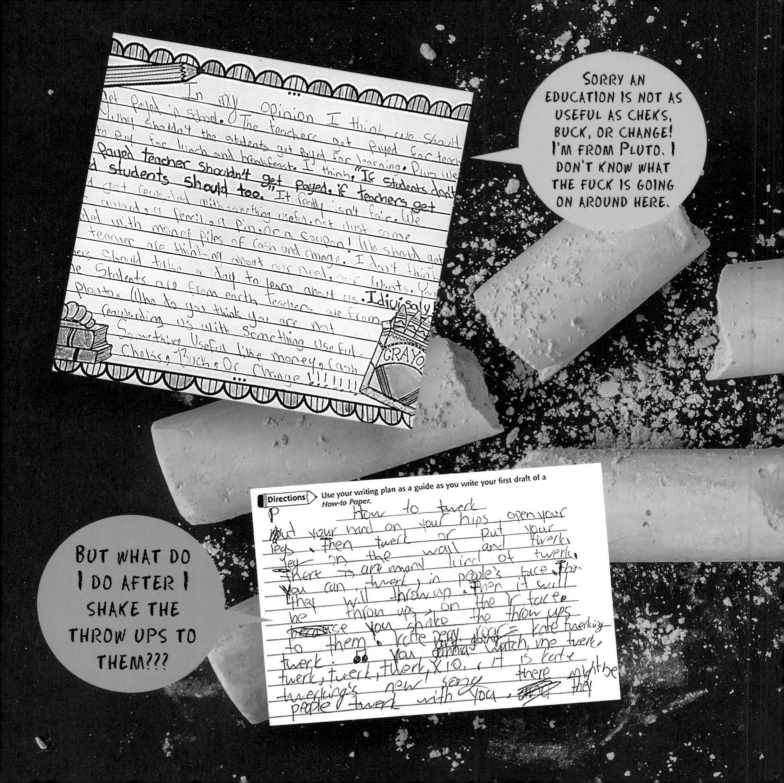

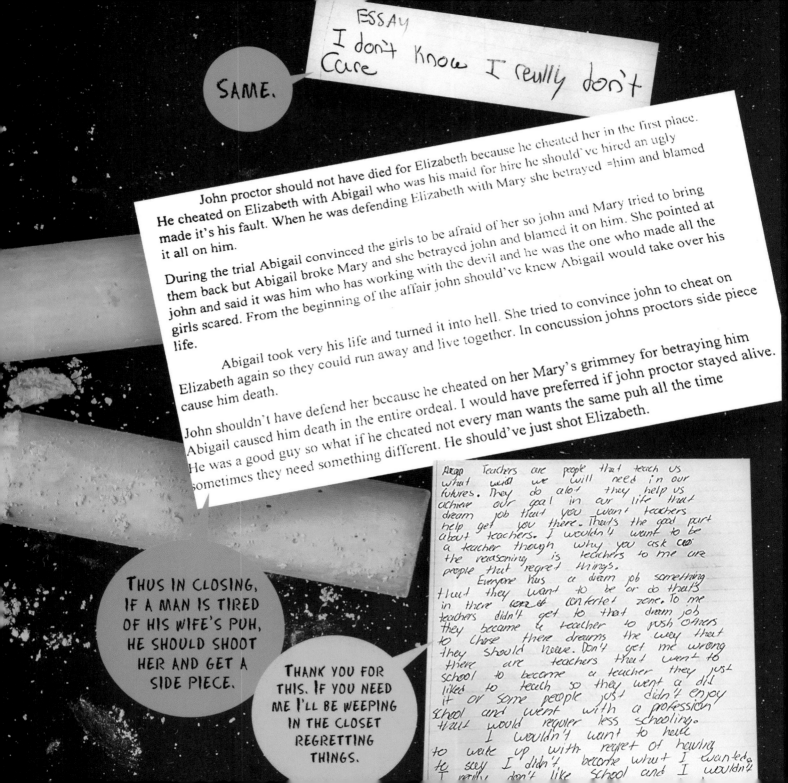

SAME.

ESSAY
I don't Know I really don't Care

John proctor should not have died for Elizabeth because he cheated her in the first place. He cheated on Elizabeth with Abigail who was his maid for hire he should've hired an ugly made it's his fault. When he was defending Elizabeth with Mary she betrayed =him and blamed it all on him.

During the trial Abigail convinced the girls to be afraid of her so john and Mary tried to bring them back but Abigail broke Mary and she betrayed john and blamed it on him. She pointed at john and said it was him who has working with the devil and he was the one who made all the girls scared. From the beginning of the affair john should've knew Abigail would take over his life.

Abigail took very his life and turned it into hell. She tried to convince john to cheat on Elizabeth again so they could run away and live together. In concussion johns proctors side piece cause him death.

John shouldn't have defend her because he cheated on her Mary's grimmey for betraying him Abigail caused him death in the entire ordeal. I would have preferred if john proctor stayed alive. He was a good guy so what if he cheated not every man wants the same puh all the time sometimes they need something different. He should've just shot Elizabeth.

THUS IN CLOSING, IF A MAN IS TIRED OF HIS WIFE'S PUH, HE SHOULD SHOOT HER AND GET A SIDE PIECE.

THANK YOU FOR THIS. IF YOU NEED ME I'LL BE WEEPING IN THE CLOSET REGRETTING THINGS.

Teachers are people that teach us what will we will need in our futures. They do a lot they help us achieve our goal in our life that dream job that you want teachers help get you there. That's the good part about teachers. I wouldn't want to be a teacher though why you ask the reasoning is teachers to me are people that regret things.

Everyone has a dream job something that they want to be or do that's in there comfort zone. To me teachers didn't get to that dream job they became a teacher to push others to chase there dreams the way that they should have. Don't get me wrong there are teachers that went to school to become a teacher they just liked to teach so they went a dif it or some people just didn't enjoy school and went with a profession that would require less schooling.

I wouldn't want to have to wake up with regret of having to say I didn't become what I wanted to I really don't like school and I wouldn't

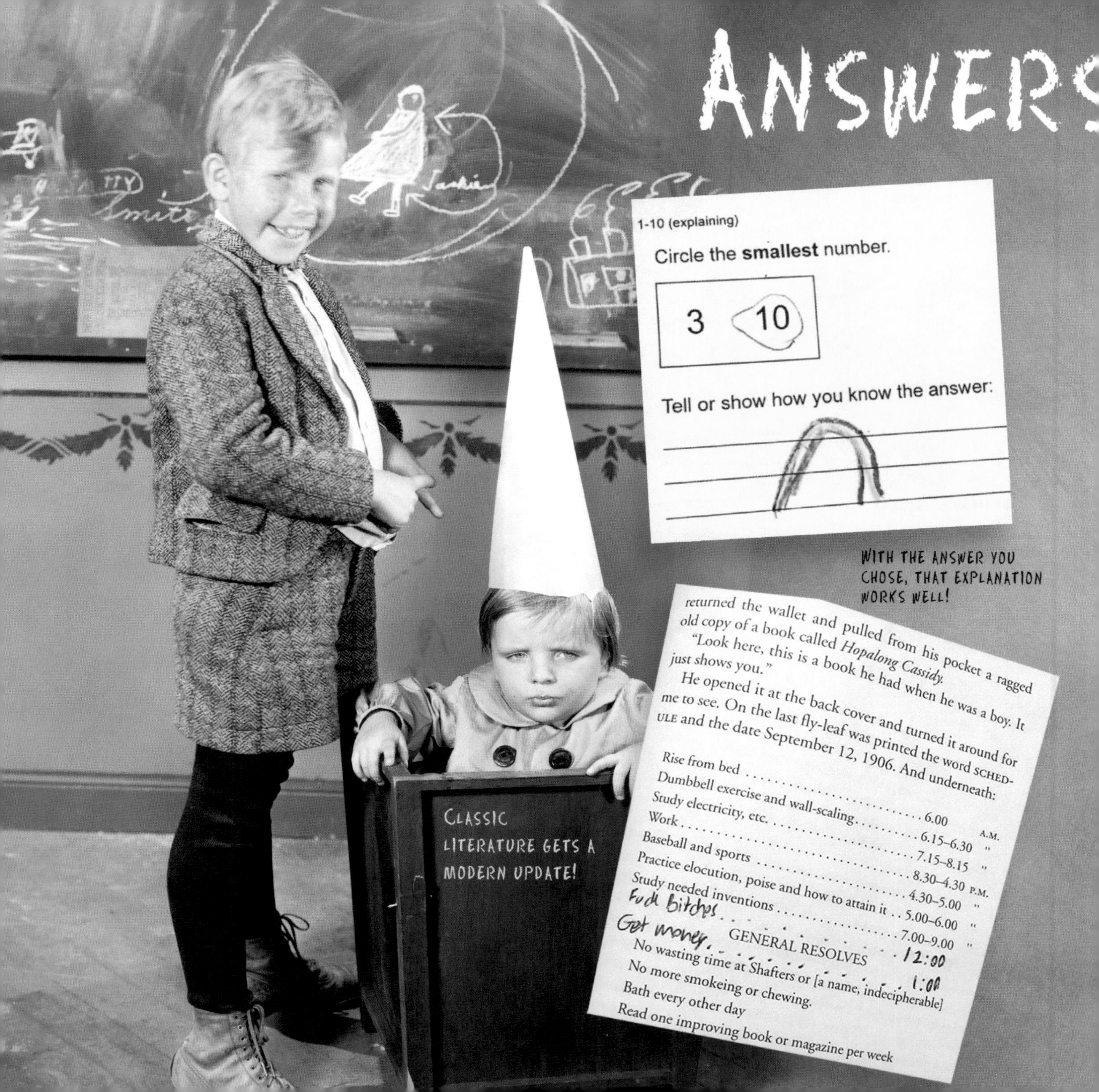
ANSWERS
1-10 (explaining)
Circle the **smallest** number.
3 10
Tell or show how you know the answer:
WITH THE ANSWER YOU CHOSE, THAT EXPLANATION WORKS WELL!
CLASSIC LITERATURE GETS A MODERN UPDATE!

returned the wallet and pulled from his pocket a ragged old copy of a book called *Hopalong Cassidy.*

"Look here, this is a book he had when he was a boy. It just shows you."

He opened it at the back cover and turned it around for me to see. On the last fly-leaf was printed the word SCHEDULE and the date September 12, 1906. And underneath:

Rise from bed	6.00	A.M.
Dumbbell exercise and wall-scaling	6.15–6.30	"
Study electricity, etc.	7.15–8.15	"
Work	8.30–4.30	P.M.
Baseball and sports	4.30–5.00	"
Practice elocution, poise and how to attain it	5.00–6.00	"
Study needed inventions	7.00–9.00	"
Fuck bitches	12:00	
Get money	1:00	

GENERAL RESOLVES

No wasting time at Shafters or [a name, indecipherable]
No more smokeing or chewing.
Bath every other day
Read one improving book or magazine per week

Crocs are an effective contraceptive because nobody wants to have sex with someone wearing crocs

THIS IS 100% TRUE AND VERY OBSERVANT OF YOU! THE PROBLEM IS PEOPLE WHO WEAR CROCS BEING ATTRACTED TO EACH OTHER!

YES, THOSE DO RHYME. GREAT JOB.

trik

thik chik

lick

lick

Look it up in your dictionary. What's the definition?

The women was prerplexed about what ove to do with my huge penis

I SEE YOU USED WOMEN INSTEAD OF WOMAN, AND I AM VERY IMPRESSED, AND WORRIED.

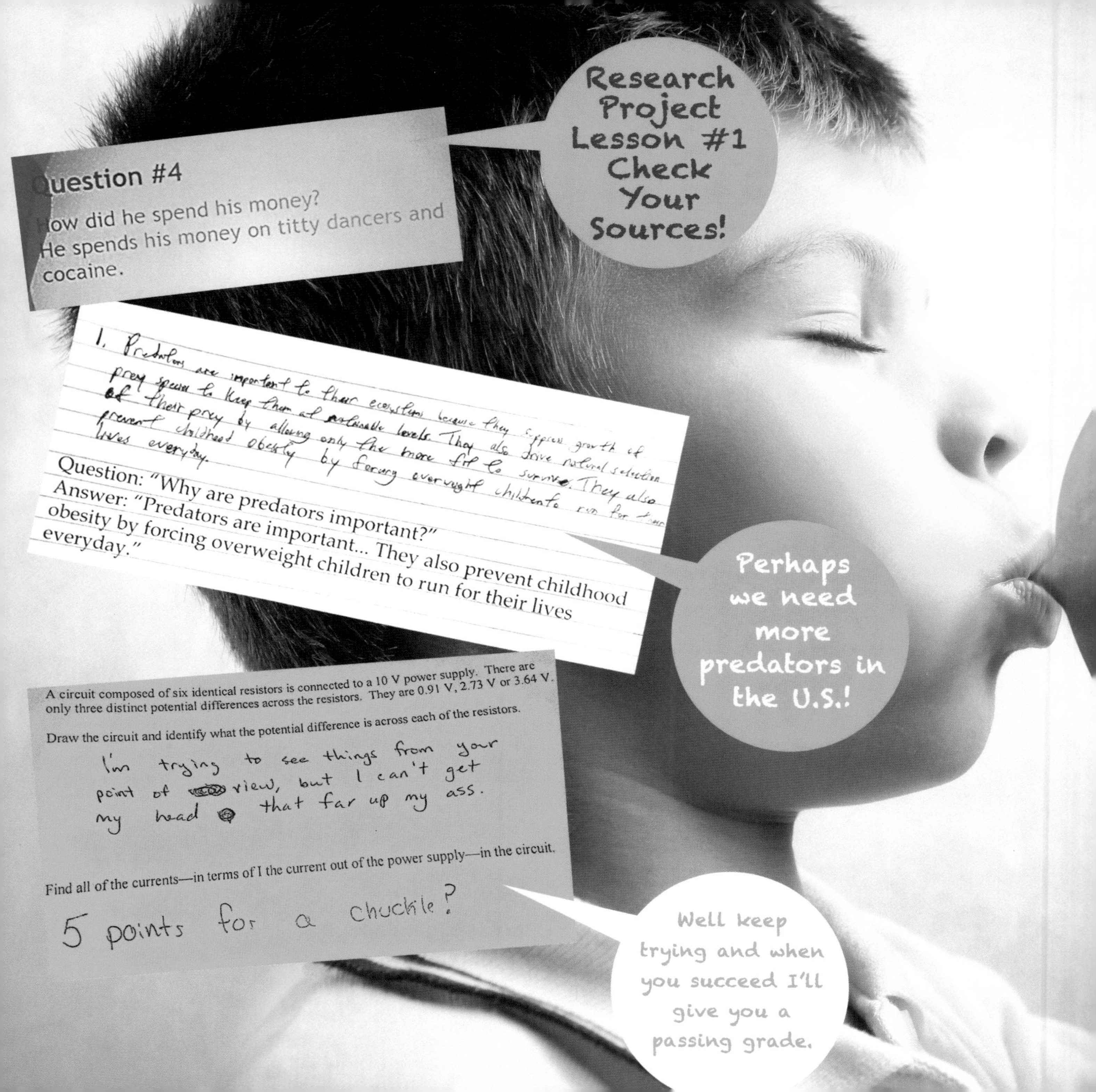

Research Project Lesson #1 Check Your Sources!
Question #4
How did he spend his money?
He spends his money on titty dancers and cocaine.
1. Predators are important to their ecosystems because they suppress growth of prey species to keep them at sustainable levels. They also drive natural selection of their prey by allowing only the more fit to survive. They also prevent childhood obesity by forcing overweight children to run for their lives everyday.
Question: "Why are predators important?"
Answer: "Predators are important... They also prevent childhood obesity by forcing overweight children to run for their lives everyday."
Perhaps we need more predators in the U.S.!
A circuit composed of six identical resistors is connected to a 10 V power supply. There are only three distinct potential differences across the resistors. They are 0.91 V, 2.73 V or 3.64 V.
Draw the circuit and identify what the potential difference is across each of the resistors.
I'm trying to see things from your point of view, but I can't get my head that far up my ass.
Find all of the currents—in terms of I the current out of the power supply—in the circuit.
5 points for a chuckle?
Well keep trying and when you succeed I'll give you a passing grade.

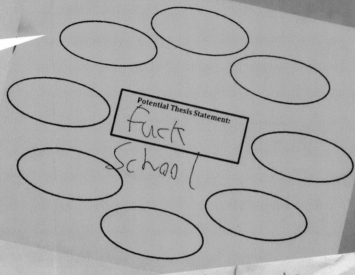

Marcus is the strongest kid in second grade. He used to lift 12 pounds. Now he can lift 97 pounds.

How much more can he lift now?

Marcos is on steroids

This detail is far more important than the math problem. Get Marcus some help!

Inaccurate! They provide excellent support for lifting the tiny ones!

62
56

11. 8/20
−16
4

There are 43 girls trying out for cheerleading. Each cheerleading squad will have exactly 8 girls. How many girls will not make a cheerleading squad?

The fat ones

NBT.7

y has four dimes. Amy has 30 pennies. Which child has more

Bobby ✓

w do you know? Show your thinking.

Precise depiction of you thinking about Bobby.

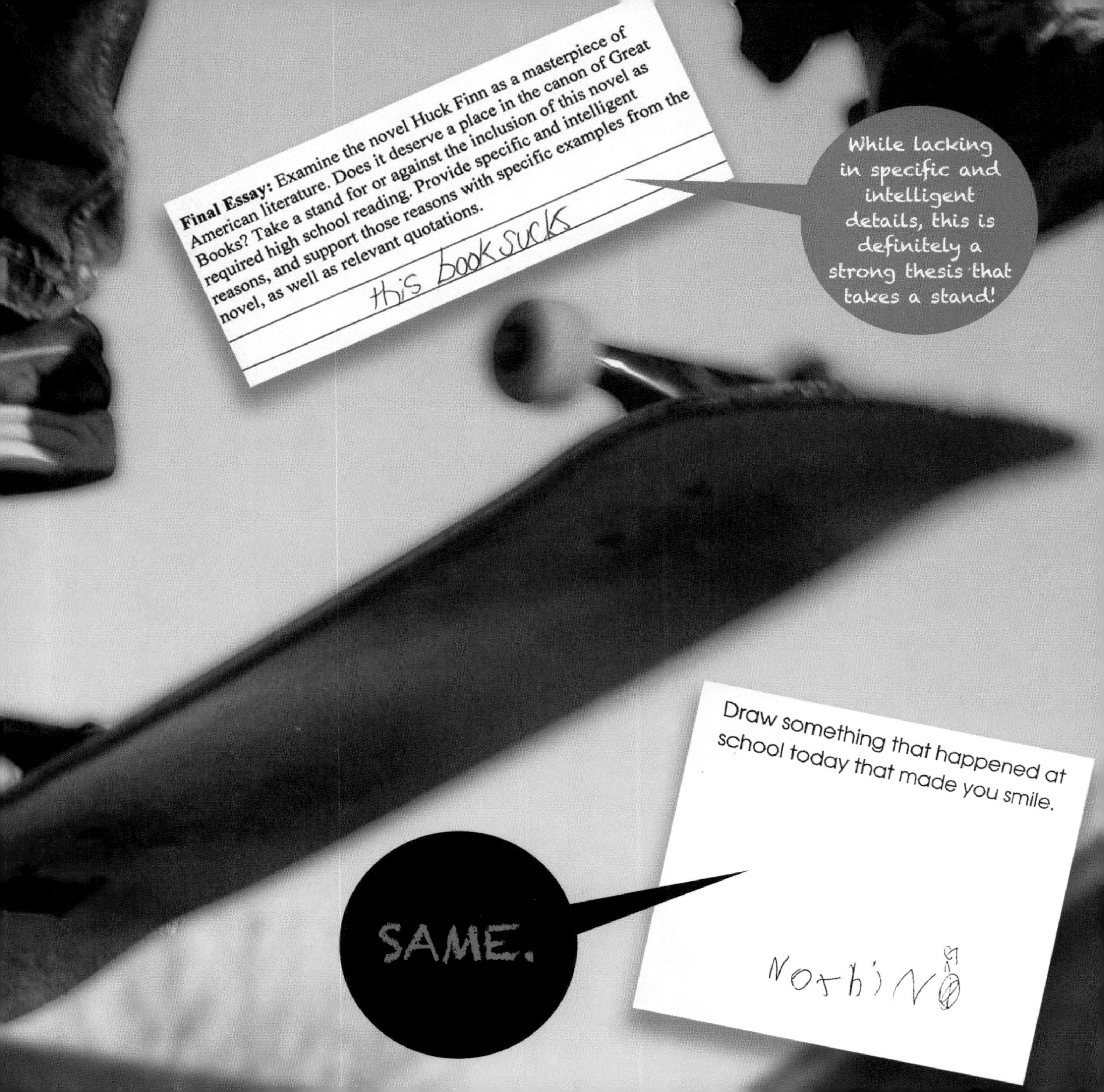

Final Essay: Examine the novel Huck Finn as a masterpiece of American literature. Does it deserve a place in the canon of Great Books? Take a stand for or against the inclusion of this novel as required high school reading. Provide specific and intelligent reasons, and support those reasons with specific examples from the novel, as well as relevant quotations.
this book sucks
While lacking in specific and intelligent details, this is definitely a strong thesis that takes a stand!
Draw something that happened at school today that made you smile.
Nothing
SAME.

drink

Trace and write the word. Say it out loud as you write.

drink

drink

Complete the sentence by writing the word in the blank.

drink plenty of water when you exercise.

Write a sentence with the word **drink**.

My mom drink's HinSey.

Mommies need their mommy juice kid!

WHAT talents do you have ?

NO

Just no.

What can you say if someone asks you to try an illegal drug?

No thank You I will take it at home

Politely ask for a to-go bag!

Questions for Thought

1. What is one thing you want to do before you die?

   tWinS

Clever yet nauseating.

The symbol I choose for myself is a goat bc im the mothafuckin Greatest Of All Time!!!!!!!

And most inappropriate of all time as well!

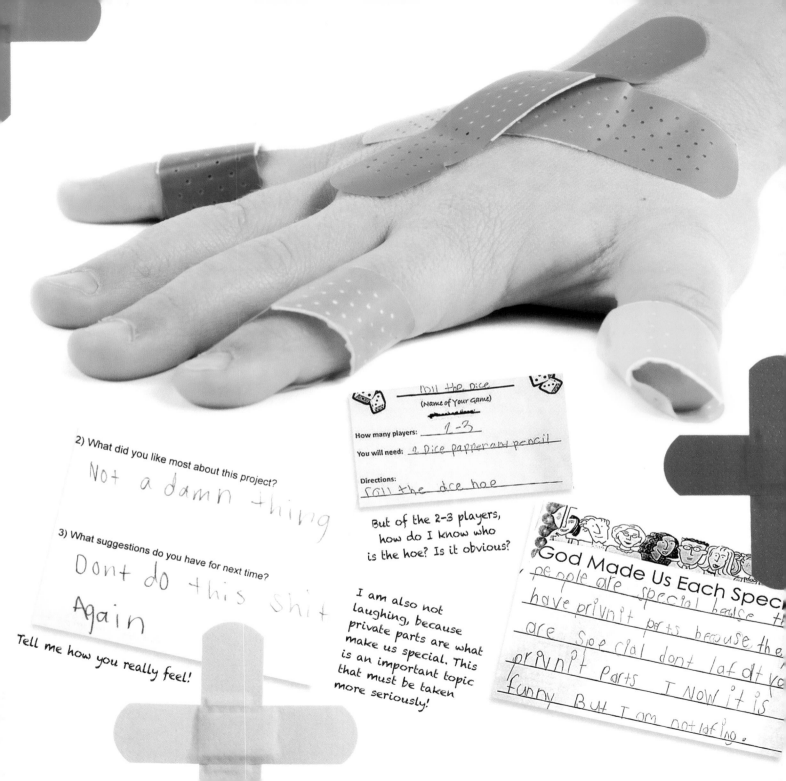

2) What did you like most about this project?

Not a damn thing

3) What suggestions do you have for next time?

Dont do this shit

Again

Tell me how you really feel!

roll the Dice

(Name of Your Game)

How many players: 2-3

You will need: 2 Dice papper any pencil

Directions:
roll the dce hae

But of the 2-3 players, how do I know who is the hoe? Is it obvious?

I am also not laughing, because private parts are what make us special. This is an important topic that must be taken more seriously!

God Made Us Each Spec

people are special beause th
have privnit parts because they
are sioecial dont laf at yo
privnit parts I Now it is
funny But I am not lafing.

I am dum I am

I AM

I am

INCIDENT REPORT

4th	5/22	████████	3
Grade	Date	Teacher	Period

When asked what he was doing (he was on the floor under his desk) he responded "your Mom"

I WOULDN'T BE MAD. KID IS QUICK!

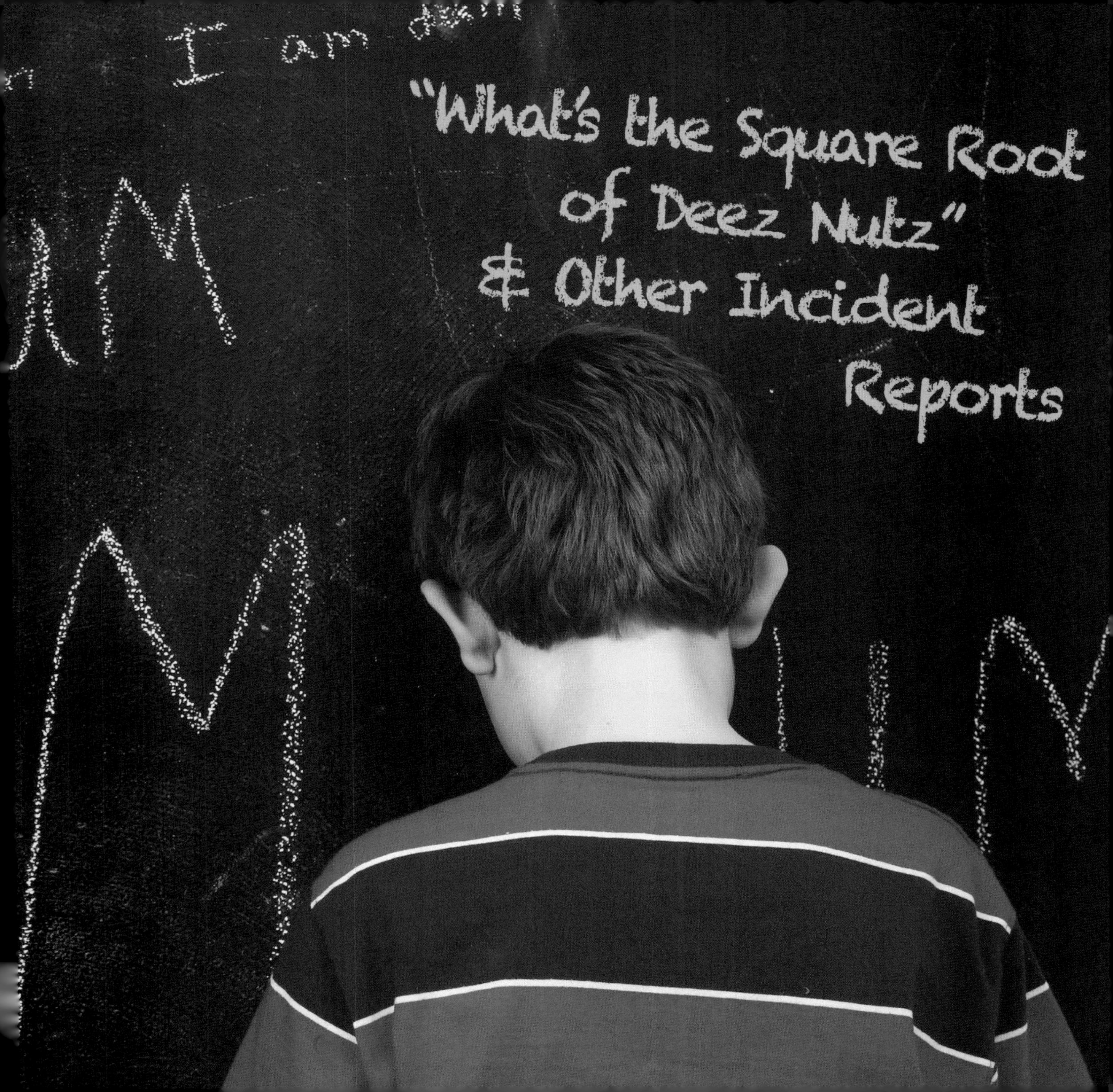
"What's the Square Root of Deez Nutz" & Other Incident Reports

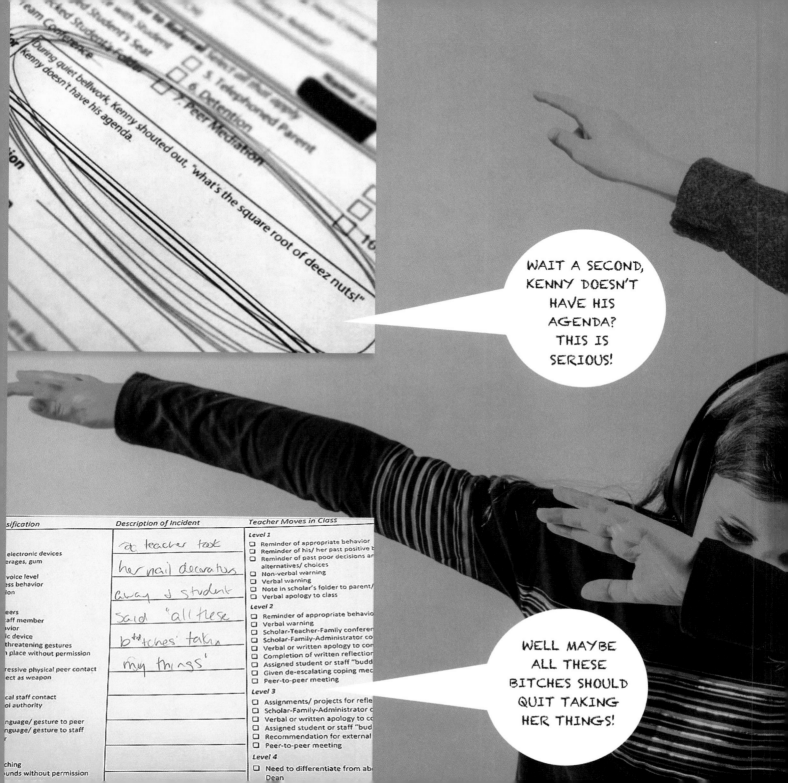

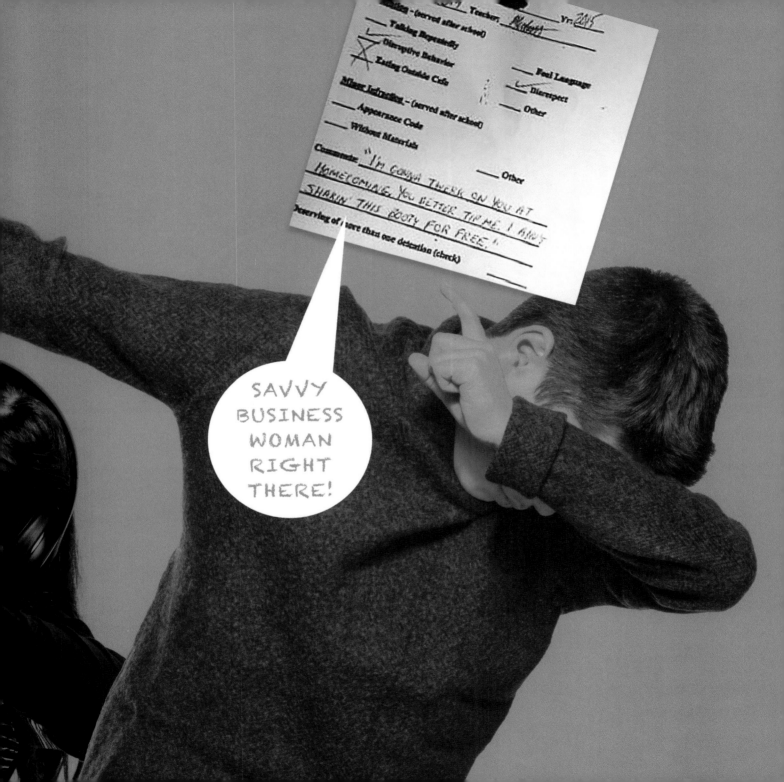

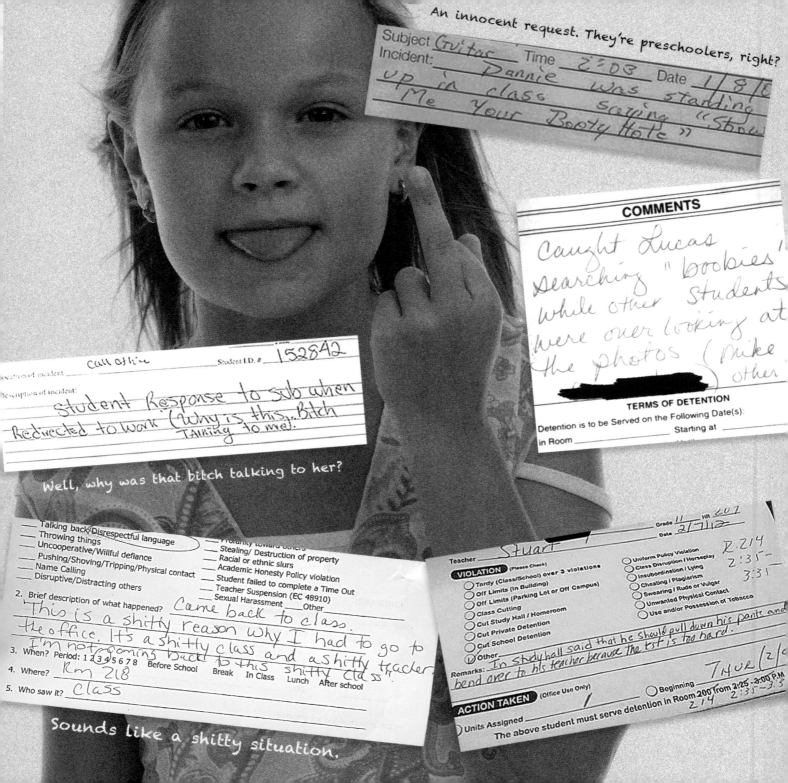

An innocent request. They're preschoolers, right?

Well, why was that bitch talking to her?

Sounds like a shitty situation.

Nature of the Problem

- [x] Classroom Discipline
- [ ] Campus Discipline   [ ] Absences: #_____
- [ ] Attendance: [ ] Tardies: #_____
- [ ] Other_____

Explanation of the Problem:
Tutor asked if she needed help – she replied.
"Don't look at me bitch"

So I guess you won't be needing any help then?

Hey, what happens outside of school stays outside of school!

Grade: 8   Date: 6/18   Period/Time:

Referral Initiated by: ████████

(This side for teacher/staff use)

Reason for Referral

shouted "Fuck school" in front of the principal as he was walking home

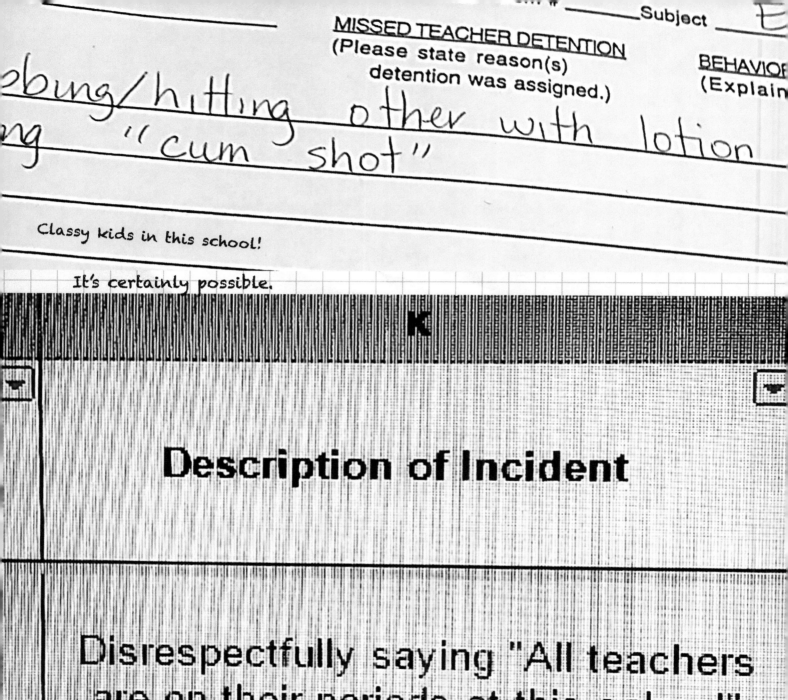

_____ _____ Subject _____

MISSED TEACHER DETENTION
(Please state reason(s)
detention was assigned.)

BEHAVIOR
(Explain

ebing/hitting other with lotion

ng "cum shot"

Classy kids in this school!

It's certainly possible.

K

Description of Incident

Disrespectfully saying "All teachers
are on their periods at this school"

Somtimes I can hear Daddy and Bich wrestling. I can tell hes winning because of the sounds she makes.

Go Dad!

Yes, parents usually wish to keep the details of those wrestling sessions private.

Do you prefer Elmer's or the standard store brand?

I like to eat

GLUE STICK

Classroom

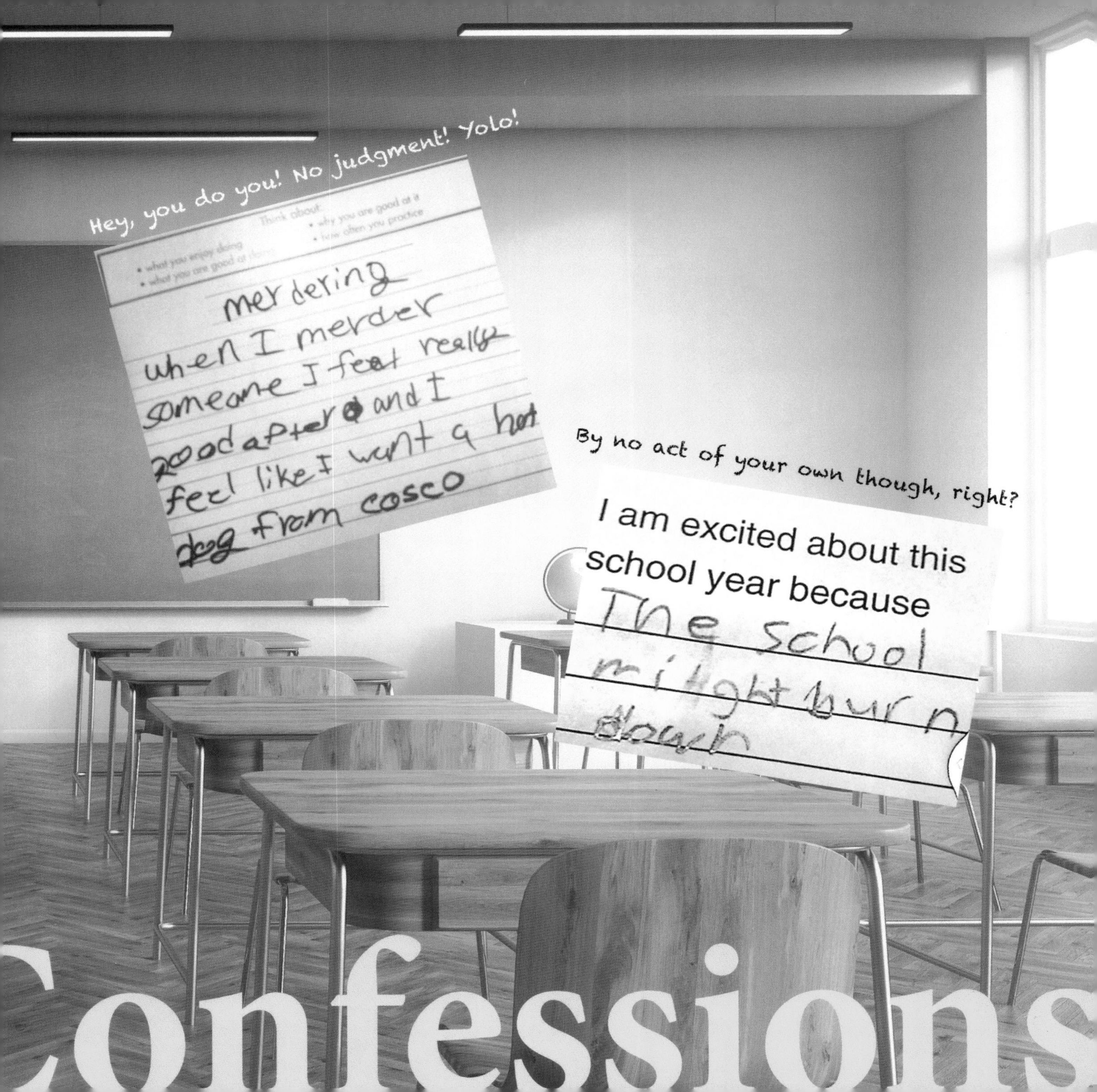
Hey, you do you! No judgment! Yolo!
Think about:
• what you enjoy doing
• what you are good at doing
• why you are good at a
• how often you practice
merdering
when I merder someone I feel really good after and I feel like I went a hot dog from cosco
By no act of your own though, right?
I am excited about this school year because
The school mitght burn down
Confessions

But are you grounded for saying fuck or are you saying fuck in response to being grounded? The world may never know.

The Troublemaker
By Lauren Castillo

Tell about a time YOU were a **Troublemaker**, just like the raccoon in the story. Remember to show details!

you are grounded!

← mom

me

fuck

I Never drink water because of the disgusting things fish do in it

Dre

I never considered this before. Thank you for bringing it to my attention.

I fart all the time

Yes, I'm aware.

8.

alive

dead

ghost

I worry about:
The rat my dad
found dead coming
alive.

Have you seen Pet Cemetery? If not, don't.

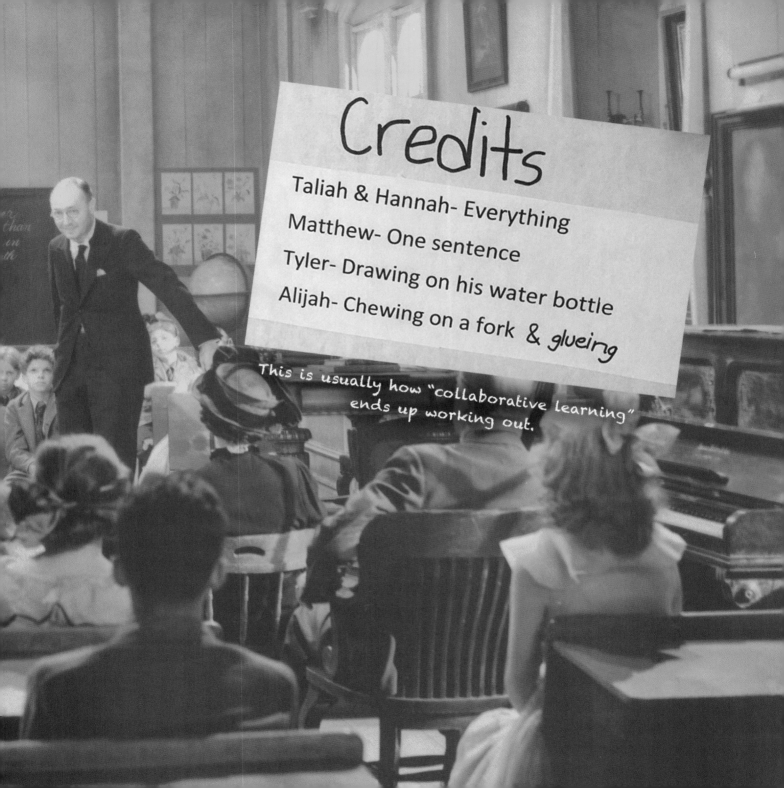

Credits

Taliah & Hannah- Everything
Matthew- One sentence
Tyler- Drawing on his water bottle
Alijah- Chewing on a fork & glueing

This is usually how "collaborative learning" ends up working out.

or Whatever

I Have A Dream

That people will give
me money so I can go
buy toys at the store.

— Liam N.

Dr. King
had a dream.
My dream is...

to work at
Taco Bell with
my Mama.

Pretty sure he didn't
mean these either.

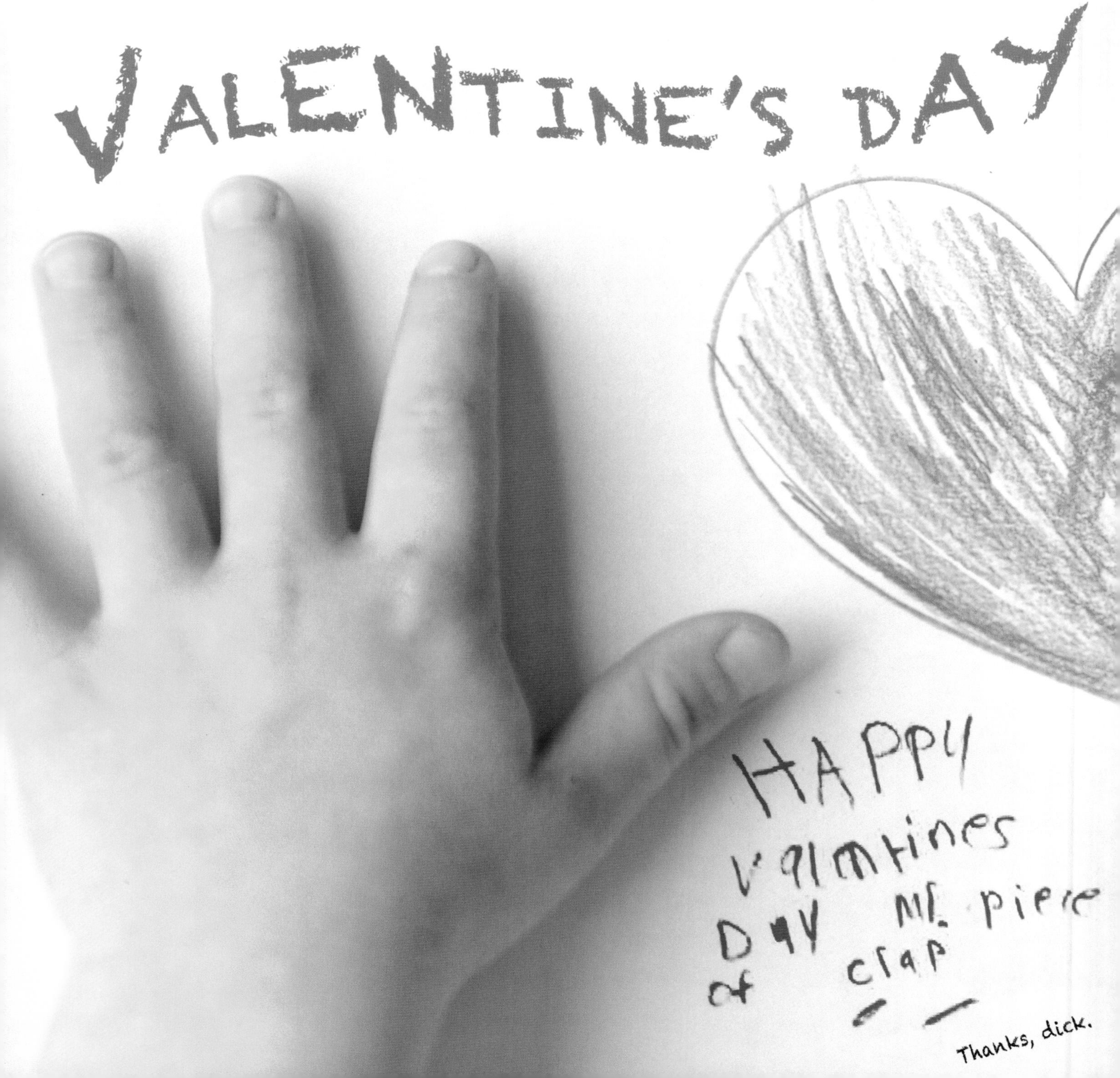

Thanks, dick.

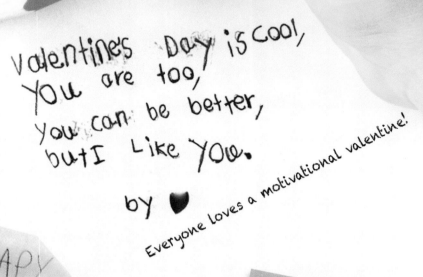

Valentine's Day is cool,
You are too,
You can be better,
but I like You.

by ♥

Everyone loves a motivational valentine!

HAPPY VAL in TITS DAY MOM

Thanks.

...from wishing you a happy **Valentine's Day!**

D: ████

From: Jonas

P.s f, hate you!! and get
out™ ©2012 The Lippy Corp. ...RDS, INC.

I never want to see you again but I do wish you a happy Valentine's Day!

MADE IN CHINA   AUG12

ST. PATRICK'S DAY

You can put them in your sweaty sack!

Sweat's for My Sweaty

Blaise

Shamcocks!

If I caoght a leprechaun I would kill him.

Does this have anything to do with Lucky Charms?

MOTHER'S DAY

She is great at cooking ___cake___

but not so good at cooking ___black ppniss___

When she is driving she ___she isn to the gun___

That's probably a good thing!

My mom always says:
fuck and shit and crap ant I love you. she says good hight. and ok.

Well, you asked!

This is what my mom does when she's not with me...
drink wine wi+ daddy

#momlife!

FATHER'S DAY

HAPPY FTES a h r DAY

Dear Dad
you may not look
handsome. But through
my eyes your all the
good dad's put
together.
from Naggolas

I love my dad,
even though he's a
dickhead.

I ♥ DAD!

2017

INDEPENDENCE DAY

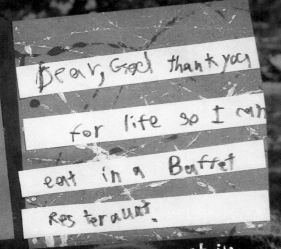

God made America so we can eat in buffet restaurants. So F you British!

Thank you solder. I totally hope you survive. America.

And I totally hope you don't die!

have a good war.

Enjoy!

Thank you for fitting (fighting) in the (war) whore.

Dear Veterans,
thank you for protecting our contry. And takeing out th enemys by shooting them in the face

Make sure you shoot them in the face.

VETERAN'S DAY

Christmas T-shirt Designs from Middle School

PEARLS

FiLL in THE SOLUTiONS

DiRECTiONS: READ EACH OF THE PROBLEMS AND COME UP WiTH A SOLUTiON FOR EACH ONE.

PROBLEMS | **SOLUTIONS**

You fell on the playground and scratched your knee. → get up and deal with it.

"Words of wisdom are spoken by children at least as often as scientists."
-James Newman

OF WISDOM

AGING

As you get older things Will seem more lame than before. Nothing Will change but you, I promise.

TEACHERS

We should respect our teachers by doing what they ask and following directions and we should respect our teachers because they might start to hate the class and quit the job.

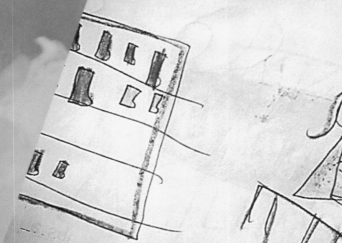

If the shoe fits... Buy it in every color,

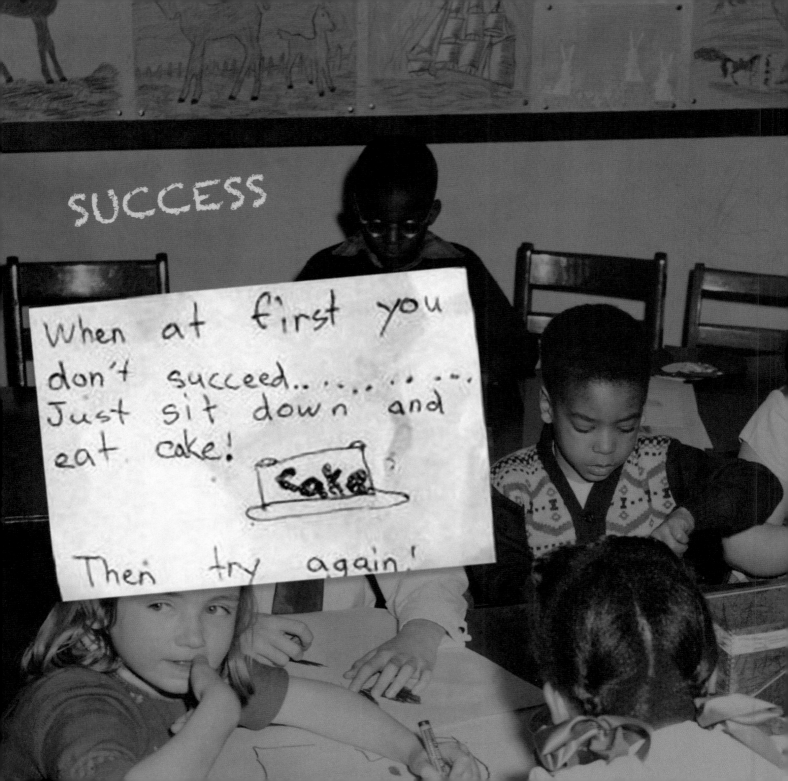

WOMEN

How to understand women.

By Cem

You Can't. The End.

Proverbs and sayings

no man.

has no turning.

never too late

Being a female is a great gift to the Universe. Here are a few wonderful things about being a girl...

We have veginas. We get jobs. We are creative. We have stuff that makes us preaner. We have milk in our bobes. We are smart. We have power.

HONESTY
Spelling
1. art
6. artless
7. prescribe
ascribe
subscribe
salary
Sorry Because of nothing

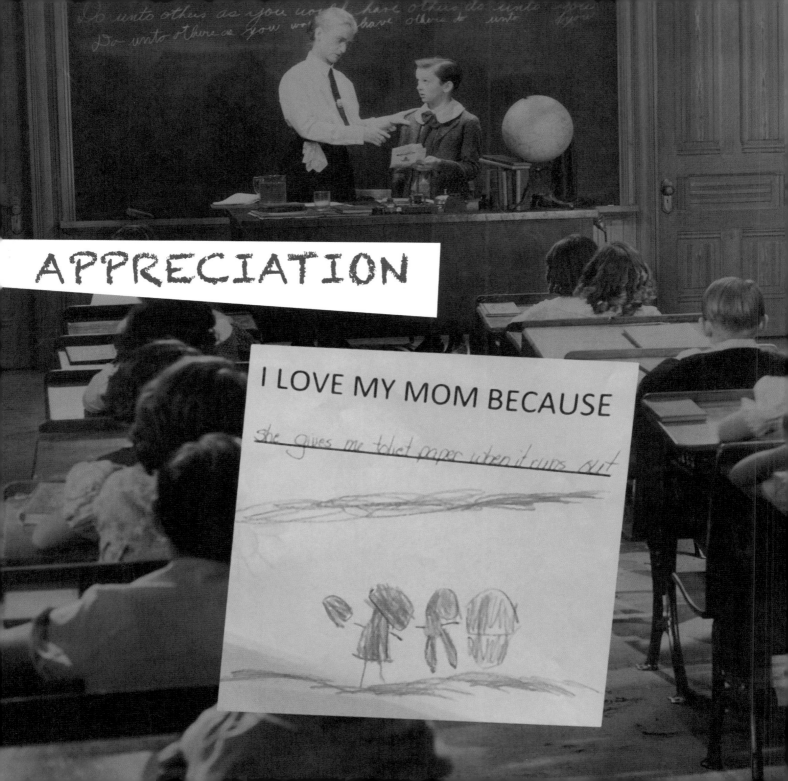

APPRECIATION

I LOVE MY MOM BECAUSE she gives me toilet paper when it runs out

FLEXIBILITY

Dear tooth-
fariy I have
bost 3 baby teeth.
can I have
~~ti~~ 9 dooler bills,
Please.
love, zelda!
P.S. I am negotiable

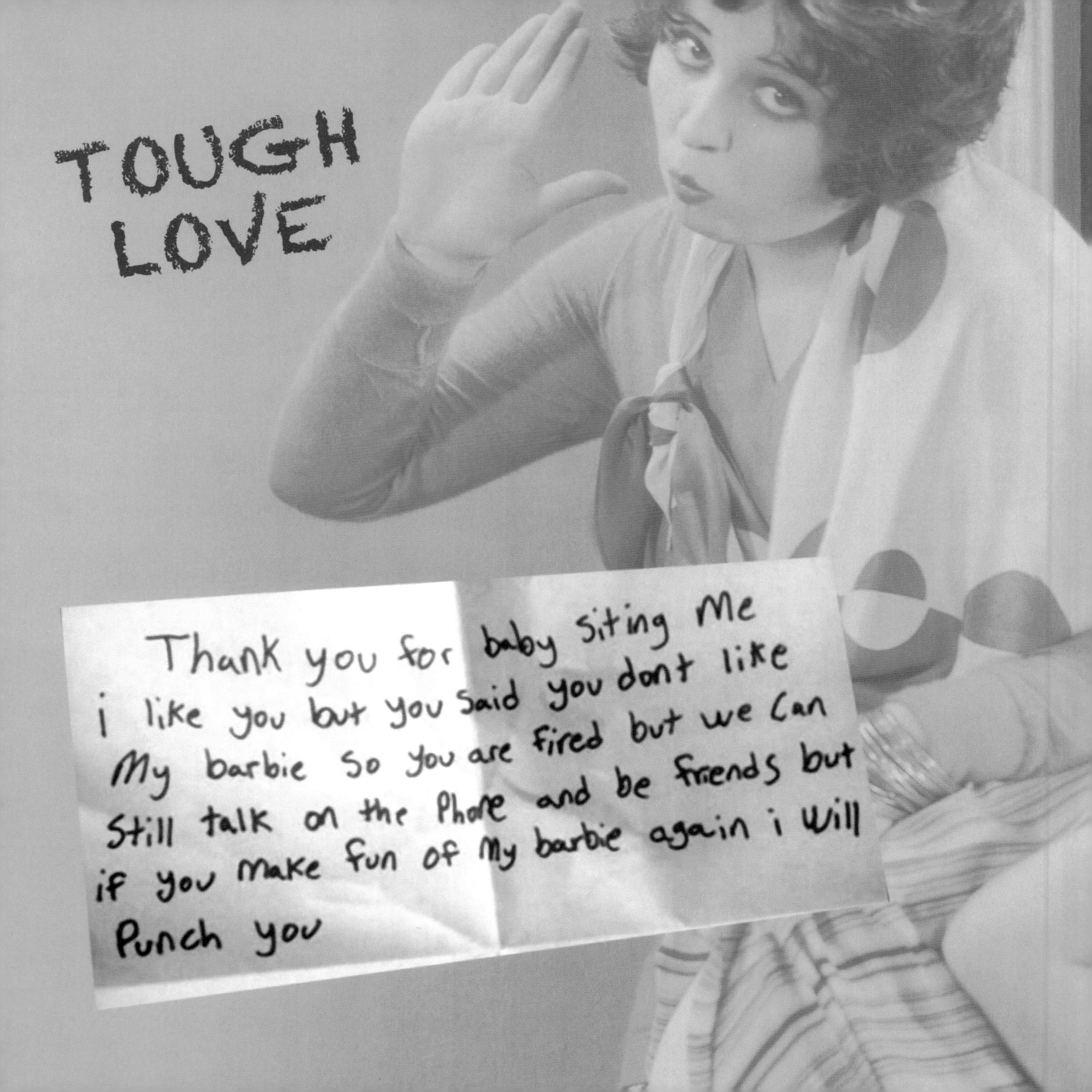
TOUGH
LOVE
Thank you for baby siting me
i like you but you said you dont like
My barbie so you are fired but we can
Still talk on the Phone and be friends but
if you make fun of My barbie again i will
Punch you

SELF-LOVE

MY HERO
One person who inspires me is:

me

ABOUT THE AUTHOR

Jane Morris is the bestselling author of *Teacher Misery: Helicopter Parents, Special Snowflakes & Other Bullshit*. She has taught English for over 10 years in a major American city. She received her B.A. in English and Secondary Education from a well-known university. She earned her M.A. in writing from an even fancier (more expensive) university. She loves dogs and trees and other things that can't talk. She has a loving family and cares about making people laugh more than anything else. Follow Teacher Misery on Instagram, Twitter, Facebook and Tumblr.

Morris as depicted by one of her students.

ACKNOWLEDGEMENTS

I would like to thank all of the teachers around the world who sent me their amazing student work! This book exists because of you. I would also like to thank my parents for my sarcastic sense of humor and my husband for understanding that I need to make fun of everything, even when I go too far.

All of my @TeacherMisery followers, you have a marvelous sense of humor and I feel like we are a family. Complaining is the best form of therapy!

And finally, I would like to thank Ian and Alan at theBookDesigners for turning my idea into a work of art!